LIFE TOOLS FOR TEENS

YOU CAN DO HARD THINGS

M. KAY BUSH, MSC SC
SCHOOL COUNSELOR

YOU CAN DO HARD THINGS
Life Tools for Teens

WHAT PEOPLE ARE SAYING

"You can do hard things is a wonderful book for making yourself better...I would recommend this book to anybody trying to change their life for the better."
—Mace, 13 year-old

"Kay has truly heard the call of what our nation's youth have needed! In her book, it's clear she has written from her heart and many years of experience working to support youth in their challenges."
—Valerie Huff, MSS, LCSW
Psychotherapist, Main Line Health, King of Prussia, Pennsylvania

"You Can Do Hard Things is a book that every teen and anyone should read to know they are more able and courageous to handle hard things...This book will change lives. It is a must-read for anyone, especially teens!!"
—Terry Sidford, TEDx Speaker, Author, Coach. Owner of Create Your Life International

"Do not be fooled by the title that suggests the book is for teens! M. Kay Bush. You Can Do Hard Things is a tool every person can use...I would recommend this book to all that want a "growing" life."
—Elda Robinson, International Best Selling author of One More Thing...

"Through relatable stories of real-life teens, Bush inspires readers to adopt a positive mindset, take proactive steps, and build resilience. The book's interactive approach encourages self-reflection and personal growth, covering topics such as goal setting, self-care, and relationships."
—Kristin Kladis, PhD
Director of Student Services, Judge Memorial Catholic High School

"Every young person should read this book. I wish I had had it when I was a teen."
—Michele Pilon, Washington Wellness with Michele Mental Health Instructor, Consultant and Coach

"Speaking from a voice that is sometimes school counselor, sometimes child life specialist, sometimes parent, sometimes teen lifts up the author's humanity as well as vast experience."
—Kristen C. Quinn, M.Ed., CMHC, CCLS
Behavioral Sciences Manager, Social Work and Spiritual Care Department, University of Utah Health

"M. Kay Bush's book was so inspiring and helped me so much with my anxiety and depression. I recommend this book to any reader who is suffering from any sort of mental illness. The great stories were so inspiring and amazing and kept me reading all the way to the end."
    —Maren, 12 year old

"Her simple, encouraging advice challenges teens to focus on what they can control, with courage, authenticity, self-care and persistence. Her eight-step tool kit and planning templates could be game changers for overwhelmed teens."
    —Mary Bolling, Australian parenting podcaster, Gotta Be Done - A Bluey Podcast

"In today's post-Pandemic- landscape, marked by heightened anxiety, social media saturation, and persistent societal divisions, You Can Do Hard Things presents invaluable resources for teenagers and parents alike to navigate challenging subjects with expert guidance and actionable tools."
    —Matthew Douglas, Ph.D. Candidate
    Dean of Students, Judge Memorial Catholic High School, Salt Lake City, UT

"Not only will it assist your teen to overcome challenges and uncover unique strengths, it will support them to meet their goals. It is a great way to assist your teenager to take charge, and become a happier, more powerful version of themselves."
   —Lyn T. Christian - Founder of SoulSalt Inc. and Best-Selling Author

"Her well-written book brings her decades of experience to help the reader become actively engaged in their journey for improved mental health. This book is an incredible tool for those that are looking for positive support as a student, teacher, counselor, coach, mentor, or parent."
   —Patrick Lambert, M.S. Ed.

"M. Kay Bush's book, "You Can Do Hard Things: Life Tools for Teens" is a must-read for anyone who is looking to reach their goals and approach life with a positive outlook."
   —Misti Mazurik, Director of Operations, RHG Media Productions

"You Can Do Hard Things" is a motivational guide empowering teens to navigate challenges with optimism, fostering resilience and courage."
   —Maureen Ryan Blake, Maureen Ryan Blake Media

"Wow! Kay has taken years of personal and professional experience and translated that into actionable items for young people, with lessons along the way. This is the book I wish I had 25 years ago!!"
—Sunny Noelle Naughton, Sunshine Silver Lining

DEDICATION

For Megan and Marisa,
May you always believe in yourselves
to get through hard things.
I know you will.

For Duane,
For always being my rock of constant optimism,
strength, and perseverance through life.
Our love and teamwork continue to help us
through all hard things that come our way.

For my friend, colleague, and children's
librarian, Linda Paoletti,
You inspired so many children through books,
and encouraged me to keep supporting young
people to get through hard things.
You are dearly missed.

For all young people who have shared their
stories with me, you are in my heart forever.
You are the inspiration for this book.
May you always remember you know
how to get through hard things.

For all young people facing life's challenges--I believe in you.
You can do hard things.

ACKNOWLEDGEMENTS

Thank you. Thank you. Thank you.

I sincerely thank everyone who helped me along this book journey.

To my husband, daughters, family, friends, and colleagues.

Thank you for your constant support and encouragement. Your enthusiasm for this book has meant everything to me.

To Bridget Cook-Burch, my lifetime friend.

Your expertise as an author, writing coach, and inspirational mentor has gone above and beyond to help me uncover my voice and share my message. I am so grateful to you for sharing this journey with me.

To Hannah Rose Lyon.

Thank you for your expert editing skills, but mostly for your gentle, yet professional recommendations. You are exactly who I needed for this process.

To the Inspired Legacy Publishing team.

Thank you Rebecca Hall Gruyter, Chisom Ezeh, Misti Mazurik, and all the team for all of your expertise and support to help me bring this book to life for the world.

To the beta readers and others who reviewed the many drafts of my manuscript.

Thank you for your input, feedback, and reviews that helped the book's message shine.

To the many young people who shared their stories with me throughout the years. Thank you for teaching me how to get through tough life challenges.

You are the inspiration for this book.

CONTENTS

What People Are Saying 3

Dedication 9

Acknowledgements 11

Disclaimer 15

My Letter to You 19

About the Paths 31

About your Parents or Guardians 37

Chapter One - Tool #1
You Can . . . Have Courage! 41

Chapter Two - Tool #2
You Can . . . Be Real! 63

Chapter Three - Tool #3
You Can . . . Take Charge! 79

Chapter Four - Tool #4
You Can . . . Keep Trying . . . And Trying! 95

Chapter Five - Tool #5
You Can . . . Take Care of Yourself! 111

Chapter Six - Tool #6
You Can . . . Ask for Help! 135

Chapter Seven - Tool #7
You Can . . . Begin Again! 153

Chapter Eight - Tool #8
You Can . . . Create Your Life! 169

You Can . . . Talk With Your Parents! 187

My Letter to Parents 193

About the Author 199

Reviews 201

YOUR LIFE TOOLKIT:

Tool #1
Have Courage

Tool #2
Be Real

Tool #3
Take Charge

Tool #4
Keep Trying...and Trying

Tool #5
Take Care of Yourself

Tool #6
Ask for Help

Tool #7
Begin Again

Tool #8
Create Your Life

DISCLAIMER

The stories I share within this book are based on the real stories of the many young people I have met through the years or who submitted their stories through the You Can Do Hard Things project at www.youcando-hardthings.today. The stories have been modified for details and identifying information to protect privacy. I honor the confidential space where these young people felt safe to share about the hard things in their lives. To explain the eight tools in this book, their stories demonstrate best how the tools work in real life. For this book, these young people are your teachers.

My two adult daughters have given me permission to share some of their experiences in this book. Through their childhoods and into their adult lives, as they have faced their own challenges, they keep learning and traveling their unique and adventurous paths. They are beautiful and brave people-- I am blessed and grateful to be their mother. When I became their mother, I discovered a stronger me and realized the tremendous responsibility I carried to raise them. They taught me how to be strong.

I knew this quote by Bob Marley was meant for me when I came across it.

"You never know how strong you are until being strong is the only choice you have."

Motherhood has been one of my hard life challenges. I have fully embraced and cherished every moment. This experience is where I have learned the incredible lessons and gifts of courage, strength, resilience, faith, and unconditional love.

I will also share some of my own stories from my childhood where I faced my own hard things. It is highly likely this is the book I needed when I was a teen, and I wish I had it then.

So, I wrote it for you now.

MY LETTER TO YOU

"Until you believe in yourself, I will believe in you."
—MKB

Dear Teen,

This book is for you if you have ever experienced anything hard in life.

It *can* feel better. You *can* feel stronger. You *can* find your way.

This book is for you if you want to prepare a successful life path.

Learn about the eight *Life Tools* within this book, and you will uncover your strengths to get through those hard things. You will see how you can direct your own life path, reach goals, and find greater happiness. This book is all about what YOU CAN DO to make a difference in your life.

What are "the hard things in life"?

They are any of the things that are hard in YOUR life.

There is no universal ruler for measuring difficulties, challenges, or obstacles. You are the only person who gets to determine if something is hard. You are your own unique and individual being.

Nobody else is YOU.

Nobody else is living your life.

It is your job to figure YOU out.

This is your life path.

Hard things may be challenges–but not limited to–anything related to school, family, your social, emotional, physical health, mental health, poverty, addiction, abuse, or trauma. You cannot compare your tough situation with someone else's, and they cannot compare theirs with yours. Do not minimize a difficult challenge. If you are feeling afraid, stressed, worried, or find that this "hard thing" is getting in the way of your happiness—that is real—and it is okay to acknowledge it.

Even though nobody wants bad things to happen in life, they happen. However, I can promise you, it is exactly in these challenging times where you will find greater strength and growth. How you react or learn ways to get through a tough situation will make all the difference. It is useful to have a toolkit of sorts that will minimize the length of time you struggle and maximize your success in reaching your goals.

In this book, you will learn tools that will strengthen and empower you, help you get focused, and encourage you to keep going despite any hard challenges that may come your way.

You will learn how to get out of your own way when you realize you are holding yourself back, limiting yourself, or afraid to show up as your true self. You will learn concrete strategies that will help you live a healthier life and manage the big feelings of hard things that will inevitably come up.

BELIEVE IN YOURSELF.

You must always believe you will get through the struggles—no matter what. You must always believe there are viable solutions that maybe you do not see yet. Keep believing there are solutions and a path to move forward, even if it is just one small step. That small step will lead to the next small step . . . and so on. When you believe you will find a solution or step forward, I promise, you will immediately feel more control over the tough situation. Begin with this mindset: *I can do this*.

Notice when you have this positive mindset. Build on it. Give yourself credit. Pat yourself on the back. This is you getting stronger.

Notice the tools you may already use to get through hard things. Reflect about a tough situation you've experienced and identify what helped you get through it.

Was it a positive mindset?

How did you put forth a little more effort and not give up?

How did you find courage and grit to keep going?

Did you take a deep breath and try again after you failed the first time . . . or the second time . . . or more?

What else may have helped you? Did you make a plan, revise a plan, or establish a new routine? Did you encourage yourself by saying positive affirmations? Did you ask for help? Did someone else encourage you?

Notice everything and acknowledge even the smallest progress. It may likely be your small efforts that made all the difference in getting through the tough situation. If you are having trouble noticing these successes, ask a friend, loved one, or trusted adult to help you see your strengths. They may be right in front of you!

Believing in yourself and noticing what you are doing well are your first tools to get through challenges and grow from them. Keep reading further to learn the rest of the tools. Read stories of teens who showed me how they found their strength and tools to get through hard things in their lives.

I have been listening to young people for a long time.

I've heard a lot of stories.

I hold every story in my heart.

I have been touched by every young person in front of me.

They have taught me about life and how to get through hard things.

While each of the following stories is unique to that person, you may relate to any of them. I hope their experiences will inspire you to keep trying and to face the challenges in your own life. At the very least, I hope for you to feel reassured that as we all face hard things in our lives, we can all find our way to learn, grow, and keep moving forward.

I started listening to these stories as a college student and child life assistant working in the local children's hospital. The enormity of the challenges the children were facing was overwhelming. Desperately, I wanted them to feel any reprieve from what was often tremendous pain, fear, and uncertainty. I especially wanted them to experience just a few moments of childhood happiness.

How could I possibly help these young patients who were facing so much?

How could I help fifteen-year-old Alicia endure the pain of spinal surgery? How could I help five-year-old Avery understand why she was urgently admitted to the hospital to begin treatment for cancer? How could I help sixteen-year-old Marcus face the year ahead, confined to the hospital, while he received orthopedic procedures on his legs? How could I help seventeen-year-old Elsa as she faced a terminal disease and would not live much longer? How could I help fifteen-year-old Amelia as she recovered from a severe brain injury following a car accident?

I knew I could not cure their cancer, change the course of a terminal illness, or change their circumstances about why they were in the hospital.

So, instead, I learned to listen, stay close, hold hands, breathe, laugh, play, cry, and *make plans*. I encouraged these young patients to identify tools they could use to get through the next medical procedure or painful episode. It all helped. They felt more control over their circumstances, and I felt useful as their guide.

These small plans and tools made a difference on so many tough days. Not knowing where my learning and future careers would take me, I did not realize at the time how valuable these tools and plans were, and how they would continue to show up repeatedly for so many teens and children in the years to come.

It was in these hospital settings where my encouragement helped Marc to create his plan to speak up more and ask questions during daily blood draws. His fears were dramatically reduced when he understood how quickly the procedure would go if he practiced the strategies of breathing techniques and listening to music to distract himself.

Young Serena was cheered on by her medical team when she bravely chose to take charge of the dressing changes for her leg following the amputation of her foot. Brock demonstrated enthusiasm to play games and tell jokes every day as he awaited a kidney transplant. He inspired everyone to keep believing, keep trying, and to begin again each day with renewed optimism for new possibilities.

These young patients were teaching me, their parents, and the rest of the hospital staff how they could take charge while they endured their exceedingly difficult circumstances. They were proving they could feel more control, stronger, and tap into their courage. It was powerful.

My plan became my mission statement and purpose.

Kay's Mission Statement:

TO HELP YOUNG PEOPLE UNCOVER THEIR STRENGTHS TO GET THROUGH HARD THINGS.

Fast forward a few decades later, and I still know I can make a difference, especially when a teen is facing some of the most difficult challenges of their lives.

This is why I wrote this book. For you.

I have witnessed, *in real life*, that these tools work!

And they will work, again, for you.

I have sat in the spaces with young people where they could have easily given up, but they did not. They found their way to keep going. You can too.

Believe you can find your way!

Choose to keep trying!

Start making your plans!

Take charge!

YOU CAN DO HARD THINGS!

The eight tools in this book will be useful now and in your adult life as well. So, why not start learning to use them now? Not only will they accelerate your growth, but they will also encourage a greater life of happiness now.

I boldly invite you to get engaged in each chapter, jump around in between the chapters, and return to reread chapters frequently when you need reminders or a reset on a new path.

Be open and honest with yourself. Notice which tools seem easy. Maybe they are tools you already know and use well. Good for you! Notice that and give yourself credit. Consider if there are tools you are avoiding or you need to learn more. Dial in on strengthening each tool and you will notice your increased confidence, resilience, and grit to face challenges. You will keep getting stronger!

At the end of each chapter, you will find pages to create your personalized action plan. This space is for you to write, doodle, or draw out your action plan. Return to these pages the next day to review what you learned—what worked or did not work. Then, revise the plan for tomorrow. Change up what's needed to be even stronger and more successful. You decide what you need to keep moving forward. You get to choose tomorrow's adventure!

1. **Today's Action: How will I show up using this tool?**

2. **Yesterday's Learning: What worked or didn't? What did I learn?**

3. **Tomorrow's Adventure: What will I keep doing? What will I do differently?**

Like life, you get to revise and change your action plan to make it work for you!

These journal pages may be the most important pages of this book, so do not skip them!

This is your space to apply the tools to your life and take charge of what is in your control.

Take charge!

Sit for a while with this book and these journal pages. Get real.

Ponder the possibilities and visualize yourself each day using these tools.

See yourself getting through your challenges and setting new goals. This is called visualization, and athletes do it all the time to get their best game on. Isn't it time to do that for yourself?

Choose to keep this as your private journal or share what you have written with someone else who will celebrate with you when they see you are taking charge of your path!

Ultimately, there are no right or wrong answers. Listen to your own gut and your own dreams. Now, let's jump into this book and journal pages together!

YOU'RE HERE...
YOU MIGHT
AS WELL
GIVE IT ALL
YOU'VE GOT.

ABOUT THE PATHS

You will see photos of paths throughout this book. There's something about how each path is unique and varied; they are winding, move up and down, have holes and bumps, but always going *somewhere*. Sometimes they connect to another path or reach a destination. Look around and there is usually another path around the corner, down the street, or on the other side of a mountain.

Path

(from Oxford Languages) https://shorturl.at/esAF7

/paTH/

noun

plural noun: paths

· a way or track laid down for walking or made by <u>continual treading</u>.

"the path continues alongside the river for half a mile"

· the course or direction in which a person or thing is moving.

"the missile traced a fiery path in the sky"

You are traveling your own path of life.

We are all traveling on our own paths. Nobody else can walk another's path. Some paths may seem similar, or travel alongside each other for a time but eventually branch off into multiple directions. For example, young families may be on one path together, students in the same grade of school may be moving together, or close friendships may be aligned with similar interests and activities. However, if you are to discover your unique, individual self, you must eventually find your own individual path.

The definition of the word states *continual treading, and course or direction in which a person or thing is moving*. Your path requires you to keep moving and to keep finding your way. Your path never ends. It keeps going, winding, climbing, around obstacles or bumps along the way.

At times in your life, you may travel your path quickly, or very slowly; it may sometimes seem to stop completely. During happy periods of your life, you may wish for time to stand still in that moment. Or during challenging times, you may pray for your path to change direction.

Embrace all points along your path and always take away learning. Remember to notice the possibilities. If you look, you will find them. If you do not see any possibilities, keep looking—they're there. Keep in mind, your path also gives you the option of turning back at any time, and that may be a good thing.

Returning to the comforts of family, loved ones, beliefs, and values can feel tremendously grounding and will strengthen you to return to and continue your journey. Of course, you decide if turning back on your path may not be healthy or helpful. If the hard things of your life are family, people, or experiences that are unhealthy, abusive, unsafe, or have caused trauma, this may be where you choose to keep moving forward to create a healthier and safer path.

*"The journey of a thousand miles
begins with one step."*
—Lao Tzu

If you take a photo of your path, what does it look like now? How do you want to travel your future path?

Keep traveling.

Keep treading.

Keep moving.

Keep finding your path.

Make mistakes.

Begin again.

The possibilities and directions you can go are endless.

Welcome to your amazing life.

ABOUT YOUR PARENTS OR GUARDIANS

Somedays, parents or guardians may get it right or they may completely miss the point. Most of the time, they are doing the best they can and are open to learning how to do better. You can help with their learning by helping them to understand you. This comes from communication both ways.

I wrote a letter to your parents at the back of the book. You may find it helpful.

How about writing a letter to your parents to say what you need to say? You'll find some ideas in the back of the book.

You are traveling your path of adolescence where you are supposed to practice independence. It can feel confusing if you're ready for it, but your parents may not be ready to let you go. Or you may not feel ready to be independent yet and you feel pressured to do more.

The reality is this likely flip-flops every day. Allow your-self some grace . . . and your parents too.

I have talked with lots of parents through the years. Most of the time they want to understand their teen-agers and support them the best they can. They are on their own path of learning life and may be facing their own challenges, which may affect you. If they are healthy and functional, it's worth it to keep them on your team.

Help your parents to know YOU. The more you share with them about yourself, interests, dreams, strengths, or hard things, they will be more supportive.

You will find some writing prompts in the section about parents at the back of the book.. They will help you get started on your letter. Go ahead and write your thoughts down. Maybe you will choose to share it with your parents—or not. That's okay! If the exercise of writ-ing a letter to your parents helps you to make sense of your relationship or how you can understand each other better, then write the letter for yourself.

What do you want your parents to understand about you?

What do you need to say?

Now, jump into the chapters of this book and immerse yourself in learning and uncovering your amazing, incredible self. See the possibilities ahead for you as you take charge and create your unique and magnificent life path. Begin now!

ALWAYS KNOW YOU CAN– AND YOU WILL–GET THROUGH HARD THINGS.

BELIEVE IT.

Take care. I believe in you. MKB (M. Kay Bush)

CHAPTER ONE

TOOL #1
YOU CAN . . . HAVE COURAGE!

*"It takes courage to grow up and become who
you really are."*
—E.E. Cummings

I don't know who I am,

I don't know why I am,

I don't know where I am,

I just know I am!

That was written by my teen self in an old journal I had saved. My evolving adolescent brain was trying to find my place in my world. I felt lost . . . but open to the possibilities in front of me.

Even at that age, I held a curiosity to understand peoples' emotions and behaviors—including my own. Growing up in a large family as the youngest child, my home environment was perfect for observing all human behavior. I quietly watched and learned from everyone.

This was an especially useful skill when I learned what behaviors would get my older siblings in trouble with our parents, fights with each other, or other questionable activities. I simply needed to do the opposite behavior!

My observation skills also revealed to me that I was missing out socially. I wanted to be out having fun with my peers. I realized that I would remain unnoticed unless I did something different. That was when I faced my own challenge: finding my courage to use my voice and make new friends.

I was a quiet, shy person but not an introvert. I loved all the activities, adventures, and social spaces. My middle school years had felt awkward and unfulfilling as far as my social life, and I was feeling a sense of doom as it continued into high school.

I was excited to get involved and meet new people. But I stopped cold in my tracks when I felt too shy to speak up and join new conversations. So, I just kept watching and observing, using the skill I had already developed from home. I saw how other kids could begin conversations and make new friends, but I couldn't do it myself. I just could not figure out how to join the groups. I was perplexed with myself as to why this had become an issue for me. I was frustrated and desperately wanted to be a part of the fun.

One afternoon, I complained to my older sister, "I'M BORED!"

She simply replied, "If you're bored, it's your fault."

BAM!

In that serendipitous moment, it was exactly what I needed to hear. I realized I had to get brave and take charge of the direction I wanted to go. I created a goal for myself, to make new friends and try new activities.

The summer before my junior year of high school, my family was moving from a small town to a larger city a few hours away. This was my opportunity to do something different—to be someone different! Rather, I would show up with the personality I knew I had on the inside. I would put my courageous face on, walk into my new school, and start talking on the first day. I would introduce myself, begin with a few conversation starters, and ask questions about how to get involved at the new school.

I was terrified but determined to make a change to be happier. I visualized myself as my true self, with an outgoing personality and enthusiasm to try new things. In the beginning, there were awkward moments where I froze, got stuck, and faded into that past familiar background I knew so well. But I became more determined as I kept seeing the end goal of possible new friends and fun. I kept trying and did not give up. I had nothing to lose and everything to gain. My courage had to show up—and it did!

Eventually, my plan worked!

I made new friends and started having more fun. The best part was I found a stronger voice and felt a new inner strength I had not felt before. I could take charge and make a difference for myself. More than anything, this experience transformed me. Speaking up and showing up as the person I wanted to be forced me out of my safe comfort zone. This required using the tool of courage. Nobody else could use this tool for me. It was my decision, and it made all the difference.

Throughout my life, I can still be a quiet person in large groups, and I still need to call on that courage to speak up. Fortunately, I also now appreciate that my quiet nature is also my strength; it has allowed me to further develop the skills of observation and careful listening. These strengths have been invaluable in my career of supporting teens, children, and families.

"Always do what you are afraid to do."
—Ralph Waldo Emerson

How has courage shown up for you?

Where do you need courage to show up now?

It is within you. Choose to use it!

I have witnessed many painful moments where teens have struggled to find their courage. They are the stories within this book, including my own. It is terrifying when you want something to be different because it could hopefully improve your situation for the better. Crossing that terror-barrier or taking that leap of faith means believing in yourself that you will be okay or even better. The only other choice is to stay where you are, but you already know that has not been working out.

Courage is where the action happens.

I know it is there for everyone, including you.

Courage shows up in many ways.

It may look like taking deep breaths before walking into school, choosing to walk away from social drama, making new friends, asking a teacher a question, sharing something sensitive with a parent, joining a club, coming out as your identity, asking your doctor more questions about your care, talking about your mental health, asking to talk with a therapist, opening up to a therapist, working out a conflict with a friend, admitting to a mistake, asking for forgiveness, offering forgiveness, or trying again at anything.

It's all courage when it comes from within and helps you get through something hard.

How do you call on your courage?

It usually starts with saying what you need to say aloud.

When a student decides to walk through my office door to talk with me, I immediately acknowledge their courage. Showing up to talk about something difficult in your life can take a lot of courage.

"Say what you need to say," I tell them. "I will listen."

It helps when you know you can sit with someone who will listen unconditionally and nonjudgmentally. I know how important a safe space is to share your most vulnerable feelings. This is when I hear the stories of hard things, and the courage to talk about them.

[Important note: some of the following descriptions may trigger something close to you. If so, please seek support.]

- This is when Luke finally felt safe to cry. His mother had just informed him that his dad had had an affair and they would be getting a divorce. His emotions poured out.

- This is when Maria told me about the sexual abuse she suffered at a younger age.

- This is when Adam told me about his father dying by suicide when he was four years old.

- This is when Lindsey, a transgender female, told me she would go the full days at school without going to the bathroom because everyone was confused about her gender. She was teased by everyone. She endured countless difficult days navigating how to fit in.

- This is when Joey told me, "My dad hits me and hurts me."

- This is when Alyce explained the reasons why she did not want to come to school. She felt extreme anxiety about being perfect, looking perfect, and doing everything perfectly. Each morning she crumpled in panic trying to get out the front door of her house.

- This is when Clara shared how she felt sad, angry, afraid, and guilty all at the same time because her sibling had cancer. She just did not know how to support her sister and manage everything she was feeling herself.

It takes courage to speak up about your feelings. But it helps when you know you want something to change or feel better. If there is something you are struggling with, talk with a trusted adult. Trust this process that it will be a start to feeling better. Once the feelings are out, you will likely feel a huge sense of release and see possible solutions and steps forward. It is always okay to ask for help. It is often helpful to have a trusted adult be a sounding board for you and will also be your cheerleader!

Throughout this process, I see teens choose an emerging take-charge plan. I may not necessarily hear these exact words from the teen in front of me, but I have frequently felt the energy in the room that says:

"This is hard,

I want it to get better,

I will keep trying.

I will keep moving forward."

I hear many expressions that are real, and it is all okay. It is always okay to say aloud how one is feeling—any feeling.

I hear:

"I can't do it."

"I don't know what to do."

"How can I possibly fix this?"

"I give up!"

Soon, I begin to hear:

"Maybe I can do it."

"Maybe there are some solutions."

"I will keep trying!"

"I won't give up!"

This is where I usually add:

"Sounds like a great plan."

"I believe you can do it."

"You've got this."

"You can do hard things."

This is where I get to see and hear incredible statements. Posture straightens, eyes brighten, and I hear:

"I can do it!"

"I will keep trying!"

"I've got this!"

"I can do hard things!"

> *"It's okay to say, "I can't handle this" for, like, ten minutes. Then decide to say, "Now, what can I handle going forward?"*

During the years of the 2020 global pandemic, I witnessed incredible courage from my students, teachers, school staff around me, and from stories I heard throughout the world. It was an unprecedented time where we all faced the challenges and stress of changes, illness, or even the deaths of loved ones.

When the school shut down, I spent my days from my home office, looking for students through the virtual world. I found students through emails, phone calls, and Zoom meetings. I listened to students tell me about their sadness, anger, fears, and feelings of hopelessness due to the sudden changes of their immediate world and the greater world. A report from the CDC (Center for Disease Control) from March 2022, showed data from the previous year, 2021. They found more than one-third of high school students reported feeling poor mental health and 44 percent reported they felt persistently sad or hopeless during the previous year, and suicide attempts increased.

The challenges of the shutdowns were overwhelming to say the least. Canceled school, canceled sports and activities, isolation from friends, canceled or virtual graduation ceremonies, parent loss of employment, family struggles, death, and illness. But it was through this adversity, where I watched up close, everyone demonstrated resilience, perseverance, and determination to adapt to the challenges. Everyone stepped into their courage. It was important and inspiring to notice the strengths that showed up during this time.

During many of the first days of the shutdown and remote school life, I needed to find my own courage. I vividly recall walking out of my little home office on the first morning of emails, phone calls, and Zoom meetings, saying out loud, "This is NOT what I signed up for!"

When I became a school counselor, I eagerly signed up to the image of sitting face-to-face with students and supporting them through hard things. I signed up to work with a team of colleagues to serve students. When the school shut down, it felt as if the rug had been pulled out from under me—from all of us. The students were no longer in front of me, and I did not know where they were. I desperately wanted to be back at school. I faced this challenge knowing I needed a plan going forward. I needed to use the You Can Do Hard Things tools for myself!

I made a plan of courage for myself. Here it is:

1. Every day I talked with colleagues, family, and friends for support.

2. I established routines at home to provide structure in my days. The most important routine I established was a morning yoga, mindfulness, and prayer session at the start of my day. This routine continues in my life today.

3. I created a schedule for my school days. This included Zoom meetings, emails, and phone calls. Our counseling team committed to a mission statement during this time. It was *to connect with students each day* (via email and phone calls). We worked tirelessly to support our students.

This plan helped me tremendously. I felt a little more in control around so much that felt out of my control. I reminded myself daily to show up with my courage.

One day, of the many endless days of sending emails to students and asking how they were doing, and pleading for them to reply to me with any response of how their days were going, I received an email from one caring tenth grade student, Molly.

She asked me, "Hey, Ms. Bush, how are *you* doing?"

I sat at my desk and cried. We were all trying to wrap around our community and take care of each other.

Every small gesture of kindness helped manage this difficult time.

Molly and I continued to talk about our days and how we were coping, realizing we both had found yoga to be a calming practice. We agreed to keep checking on each other throughout the rest of the school year.

You can find your courage to do hard things.

Make a plan.

Make a plan with small actions forward.

Begin.

You will discover a stronger YOU.

YOU CAN . . . HAVE COURAGE!

TODAY'S ACTION PLAN

Today, how will I show up with courage?

Actions for today:

_____

_____

_____

_____

_____

_____

_____

_____

_____

_____

Doodle or draw here . . .

YESTERDAY'S REVIEW

What worked—or not?

What did I learn?

_____

_____

_____

_____

_____

_____

_____

_____

_____

_____

_____

Doodle or draw here . . .

TOMORROW'S ADVENTURE

What will I do again?

What will I do differently?

_____

_____

_____

_____

_____

_____

_____

_____

_____

_____

_____

Doodle or draw here . . .

CHAPTER TWO

TOOL #2
YOU CAN . . . BE REAL!

"Be yourself. Everyone else is already taken."
—Oscar Wilde

The challenge of figuring out who you are may be the most overwhelming, mysterious, and complicated journey you will ever take. It will take a lifetime *and* it will be worth all your efforts! So, the best thing you can do now is to allow it to unfold and start noticing yourself.

It's about learning your interests, your values, your personality, and deciding to be true to those things. Give yourself permission to try new things, take adventures, and think out-of-the-box about all the possibilities around you.

You are surrounded by every message that tells you who you *should* be. Some messages may be important ones that influence you to become your best self. Faith, religion, community, family, or society may be positive messages for you, or they may be things that conflict with you. Consider all messages and how they may guide you to become who you think you want to become. Start noticing the messages from social media and advertisements that imply how you are supposed to look and act.

Question these messages!

Check in with yourself to discover if any of this is real or accurate. Observe peers and their behaviors. Notice if they are doing their own work to become their best selves, or following an assumed formula that just lumps them into "sameness" and "emptiness."

Spend time with yourself.

Get to know yourself.

Get real.

You are truly a unique individual. Whether you believe you were created by God, another higher power, or a clump of cells that mixed and became you, you are on this earth for a reason. It's your job, journey, and an incredible opportunity to figure out who you are and who you want to become. It's your job to show everyone else who you are or who you are becoming. When you choose to be real about learning and understanding yourself, you will discover a life path of greater happiness and success.

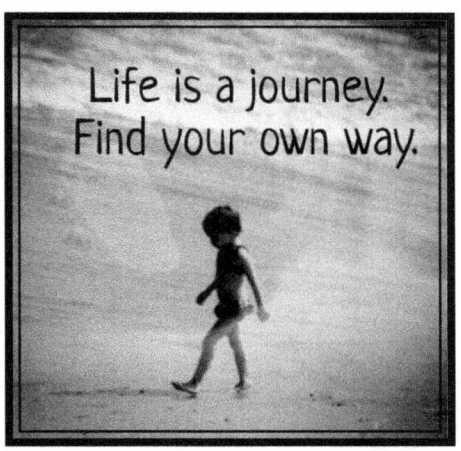

Be kind to yourself during this journey. Be kind to your peers since they are doing their own work to uncover their true selves.

Choose to be real.

Choose to be true to yourself.

Choose to be honest with yourself.

About honesty: are you being honest with yourself when you do something that does not align with your true self or the goals you want to reach?

Are you getting in your own way?

I've met a few teens who've struggled with being real with themselves. High school senior, Emma, told me in her first year of high school how she sometimes got in her own way.

"If someone tells me that I have to do something, I want to do the opposite." She went on to explain, "Even if it's something I know is good for me, like doing homework and studying for tests, I want to do the opposite."

Emma talked about her goal to graduate, but her actions of "doing the opposite" unfortunately resulted in not reaching graduation with her peers. While there were certainly other factors and challenging life circumstances that affected Emma's path, she could not find her way to take charge of what she wanted. She got in her own way.

Get real about the person you want to become.

Align your actions every day to become that person.

Dismiss outside influences that will knock you off your path. Take charge of your journey; immerse yourself in learning and working hard towards your goal. When mistakes happen and temporarily derail you, honor those mistakes as more learning, then get back on track.

"Remember always that you not only have the right to be an individual, you have an obligation to be one."
-—Eleanor Roosevelt

Blake worked hard to stay on his own path. He arrived in high school, following troubled middle school years, where he was teased because of his interests and personality. Who he was just did not click with the other students at his middle school. He was comfortable in his own skin and wasn't interested in the social circles around him. He loved to read and always carried a book.

Quiet by nature, Blake preferred to keep to himself. He carried a book to lunch period each day where he sat separately from other students, eating and reading alone. He had the same routine during recess on the playground. He would find a secluded spot on the playground equipment or at the edge of the blacktop area where he would continue to read alone every possible minute.

Sadly, many classmates decided he was a target to be teased. They mocked him during gym class because of his lack of physical skills and coordination. In the classroom, students were mean simply because he wasn't interested in socializing with them.

This cruelty from the other students affected Blake. There were days where he could not ignore the taunting, and he sat quietly crying, trying not to be noticed by anyone. But he was noticed by this school coun-selor. I asked Blake to visit me in my office. He readily responded with appreciation that he could be rescued to a safe, quiet space.

Blake expressed confusion about why he was teased by the other students. He was open to making friends but had not found anyone who shared his interest in reading and quiet conversations. He was comfortable enough with himself that he did not feel the need to put on a forced, fake facade to fit in. So, he kept to himself.

Incredibly, about mid-school year of eighth grade, two students broke away from the majority group and reached out with kindness toward Blake. It was remarkable to witness the courage of these two students, who clearly wanted something more from friendships than what they had been experiencing with the other students. Soon, Blake and his newly found friends formed a connection that continued throughout the year. Blake had stayed true to himself. His new friends respected him for his strength to be real, and they wanted to know him better.

Ironically, when Blake moved onto high school, my job position changed, and I ended up at the same high school. It was incredible to watch Blake's quiet world open to a larger social circle and opportunities. Blake quickly found peers more like him– quiet souls, readers of stories, and deep thinkers about the world.

He was validated for being himself. He found clubs and activities and thrived. He excelled academically and was recognized with awards by his teachers. He further developed his love of reading into creative outlets of art and writing. By the end of his senior year, Blake received top awards in English classes and was recognized for leadership in art, writing, and literature.

Blake had stayed the course, knowing who he was and who he would become throughout these school years. While there were many difficult moments where others did not take time to get to know him, he knew himself. He discovered an environment in high school where he could shine. He continued to learn, grow, and seize opportunities.

Are you being real?

Do your actions reflect your true self?

Give yourself permission to start learning more about yourself. If you're not sure who the real you is . . . it's okay! Start today.

Here are some ways to discover who you are:

1. **Take charge! Start trying out new activities, clubs, sports, or other interests. Notice what energizes you and piques your interest.**

2. **Take some time to journal about yourself– for yourself. Learn about YOU.**

3. **Make lists of positive qualities about yourself, your dreams, your interests, where you want to go in life.**

4. **Expand on what you discover from your lists and start setting actions to become who you want to be and where you want to go.**

Learning about yourself will take your lifetime. You will evolve as you grow up and you will get to travel many paths ahead. This is a beautiful place to begin.

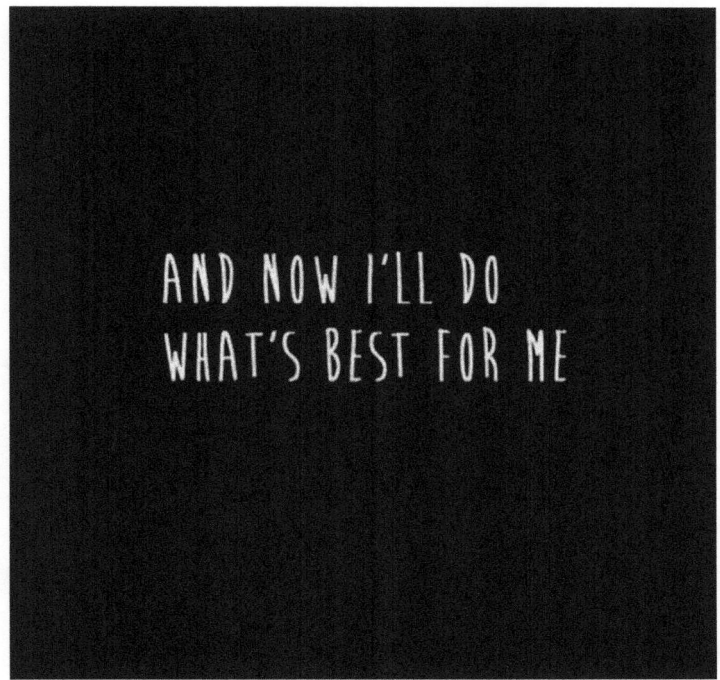

YOU CAN . . . BE REAL!

TODAY'S ACTION PLAN

Today, how will I be real?

Actions for today:

_____

_____

_____

_____

_____

_____

_____

_____

_____

_____

_____

Doodle or draw here . . .

YESTERDAY'S REVIEW

What worked or did not?

What did I learn?

_____

_____

_____

_____

_____

_____

_____

_____

_____

_____

_____

Doodle or draw here . . .

TOMORROW'S ADVENTURE

What will I do again?

What will I do differently?

_____

_____

_____

_____

_____

_____

_____

_____

_____

_____

Doodle or draw here . . .

CHAPTER THREE

TOOL #3
YOU CAN . . . TAKE CHARGE!

*"You don't have to see the whole staircase; you
just have to take the first step."*
-—Martin Luther King, Jr.

"Hi Kyle," I greeted the twelfth-grade student who stood at my office door. "It's great to see you. Come in, please sit down, and let's catch up." I motioned for him to enter.

I was happy to finally see Kyle, since he had been avoiding my emails and notes to meet with me. I assumed Kyle knew I was concerned about his failing grades, multiple late slips, and unexcused absences from many classes. He was struggling and at risk of not reaching graduation.

"Hey, Ms. Bush. I've been busy. I have a job because I need to pay for my car," Kyle offered immediately.

I followed with, "That's great; sounds like you are working hard. How are you feeling about school?"

Kyle sunk in the chair next to my desk. He knew this conversation had to eventually happen. "I've gotten behind in all of my classes and it just doesn't seem worth it anymore." His voice cracked with emotion. "There's so much to do; it's overwhelming. I know I'm giving up; I guess I don't really care about graduation."

I suspected that Kyle would like to graduate but didn't know how to recover from where he was and how to take charge to improve the situation. He knew he had stopped trying with school, and now it felt impossible to get back in the game. Worse, he was justifying that it was okay to not earn that diploma.

Have you ever found yourself in this situation?

I've met many students like Kyle. It happens. For many students, managing school, extracurricular activities, sports, jobs, and family responsibilities can be incredibly challenging. The high school years are filled with many opportunities, so it is a learning process how to manage it all.

I've seen many students accomplish this balance when they learn the skills of time management and determination. Unfortunately, if anything starts to fall apart in "doing it all," it can leave you paralyzed and stuck. It's easy to give up. However, it is possible to recover, get stronger, and reach your goals.

It begins with choosing to take charge.

At any time, ask for support from your school counselor for strategies to organize, prioritize, and schedule everything. Yes, that means using a planner or writing everything on a calendar! These are strategies used by successful people. It's worth it to start learning them now.

I asked Kyle, "What if it's possible to get caught up again?"

"Is that even possible now? I'm so far behind." Kyle looked at me with a glimmer of hope.

"Yes, it's possible if you take charge of one action at a time," I assured him. "Are you ready to take charge of one action?"

At this point, Kyle accepted my optimism and agreed he could begin with one action. First, he would meet with his teachers and start talking about how his grades could be improved. Teachers genuinely want to help students succeed. When a student asks for help, teachers truly want to help. I was certain once Kyle accomplished this, he would begin to feel connected to school again.

Kyle and I discussed strategies to support him in managing school, homework, and his job. He renewed his commitment to earn his graduation diploma. We celebrated when he reached graduation and earned his diploma. He did it!

Taking charge does not need to be an overwhelming load of tasks to reach the big, end goal. That's usually too much and will get anyone stuck; they'll never start and will likely never get finished. Instead, choose a short-term goal with small actions. Then get started with the first action, followed by the next action, and so on. Before you know it, you're building momentum and feeling in control of your life.

Take charge of small actions to move forward.

For example, let's say you have an *F* in chemistry class. An *A* feels so unreachable you might want to give up. Instead, set the short-term action to just get to a passing *D* grade. Small actions might be getting all assignments submitted going forward, improving one study strategy in preparation for the test (notecards, mind-maps, or a study group), or asking the teacher for suggestions. When you reach the passing *D* grade, set the next small action to reach a *C*. Before you know it, you'll be strengthening your study skills, increasing your confidence, and reaching *A*s!

Taking small actions have been demonstrated by many, many students I have known throughout the years, and they've found they work.

Sometimes "taking charge" simply means to walk through the school doors at the beginning of any school day. While this may seem easy for some, there are many individuals who struggle with anxiety, phobias, or trauma-related events that make this a paralyzing step.

"Always remember you are braver than you believe, stronger than you seem, smarter than you think, and loved more than you know."
-—A.A. Milne

I listened to ninth grade student, Sam, as he shared with me the gripping anxiety he felt thinking about the school day in front of him that would be filled with academic pressures and social expectations. It was too much. Many days, he could not get out of his dad's car. Some days, they sat for more than an hour outside of school, attempting to problem-solve what might help, only to give up and return home again. He was missing a lot of school days and falling behind academically.

Nothing was working. This usually increased anxiety and frustration for both of them. It was an unhealthy cycle of events that was leaving Sam less and less able to take charge of his days.

Chloe carried the stress of her home life with her through the school doors each day. Her parents were unemployed, and there was constant uncertainty on how to manage the needs of their family. Chloe had to take charge of household chores and care for her younger siblings. She was exhausted by the time she arrived at school. Her ability to focus on and participate in her high school experience was minimal at best.

In all these stories, the first action is to take charge and seek additional support.

Kyle, Sam, and Chloe eventually met with their school counselor. They wanted to feel better. Meeting with these students, I was able to help them design manageable plans with small actions that helped them feel a sense of control over their circumstances.

These are just a few small actions that can help you get through the school doors to begin the day:

- **Prepare the night before. Get organized. Wake up at a realistic time that allows you to get ready and arrive at school on time. These actions will decrease anxiety tremendously. Once this becomes a routine, it's easy.**

- **Have a conversation with your parents to ask for support and help with a plan. They will appreciate your initiative and thank you when it helps the whole household to feel calm in the morning.**

- **Once you've made it through the school doors, check in with a trusted adult, school counselor, or teacher. They will be your cheerleaders to take the next action to keep your momentum going.**

- **Breathe and visualize. Practice pausing at any step of the plan. See yourself following through with each action. Feel calm, confident, and in control. The more you practice this exercise, the more your mind and body will respond accordingly. You will feel more in control.**

- **Can you think of more strategies to take charge of beginning your days strong?**

CHOOSE
YOUR DAY...

...or someone else
will!

YOU CAN . . . TAKE CHARGE!

TODAY'S ACTION PLAN

Today, how will I take charge?

Actions for today:

_____

_____

_____

_____

_____

_____

_____

_____

_____

_____

Doodle or draw here . . .

YESTERDAY'S REVIEW

What worked or did not?

What did I learn?

_____

_____

_____

_____

_____

_____

_____

_____

_____

_____

Doodle or draw here . . .

TOMORROW'S ADVENTURE

What will I do again?

What will I do differently?

_____

_____

_____

_____

_____

_____

_____

_____

_____

_____

Doodle or draw here . . .

CHAPTER FOUR

TOOL #4
YOU CAN . . .
KEEP TRYING . . . AND TRYING!

"Everything will be okay in the end.
If it's not okay, it's not the end."
-—John Lennon

You weren't supposed to give up, I repeated in my head.
I had just heard the tragic news that a former student,
Michael, had died by suicide. It had been eight years
since I had seen Michael when he was in elementary
school. I remembered two sides of Michael. He was the
student full of energy, enthusiasm, and charm, unifying
his class to win the kickball game or to line up for lunch.
He was the first to reach out his hand to help a class-
mate in need. He took charge to silence the noisy class
when he noticed the teacher's rising frustration. He was
always polite and respectful when he visited my office.

Michael also had an incredibly sad and angry side.
A bad day or a frustrating situation could result in an
explosion. His tolerance to manage his emotions was
beyond his reach. Some days this side took over and

spiraled Michael down to a place where he needed space and support. That's when he came to my office.

He did not seem to mind that he was sent to see me when he was out of control. I allowed him to say what he needed to say. He felt safe and eventually calmed down–and then he usually cried. It was difficult for Michael to explain his anger and the incidents at school that didn't make sense to him.

Michael suffered the trauma of a lifetime of family struggles and frequently felt everything was out of his control. In those moments, I reminded Michael of his strengths to get through hard things. He demonstrated incredible grit and perseverance to show up to school every day and complete his schoolwork, along with stalwart determination to be happy. He needed these reminders of his internal strength to carry him through the difficult moments. Michael always seemed reas-sured that he had what he needed to keep trying.

I sobbed the day I heard Michael died. I will never know what was going on in his world during that time. At some point, he must have forgotten that he had what he needed to keep trying and to keep going. My heart was broken for the loss of the gifts Michael had to share with the world.

Giving up is not an option.

There are always solutions.

I promise.

There is another path for you.

You must always believe there is another idea, but you just haven't found it . . . *yet*. Ask for help. Be open to what you may need to hear from a different perspective. Be open to trying something different. Just keep trying.

Zach wanted to give up many times, but he kept trying. Zach arrived at my high school when his family moved from another state in the fall of 2020. One year later, he told me that the previous year had been the hardest year of his life. He'd learned a lot about himself when he found courage and strength within to keep trying . . . and to live.

Due to the ongoing pandemic and health isolation mandates that particular year, Zach's parents requested online distance learning. He agreed, even though it meant, as a new student, he would have great difficulty meeting students or having any kind of social life.

Every day Zach sat in his bedroom and signed into each of his classes via Zoom. He participated and engaged as much as possible. He submitted his work and did very well in the first half of the school year. He communicated with his school counselor through email and phone calls. Then, something changed.

Zach explained, "I just got tired. I didn't feel like I could sign in or do any assignments. I didn't even feel like I could leave my bedroom. I didn't want to go outside. I was worried about getting sick."

Not long after that, he stopped responding to emails from his teachers and school counselor and was failing all his classes. He became aware of conversations that were happening between his parents and school counselor. Everyone was concerned. Zach told me he felt increasingly unable to interact with anyone. He stayed in his bedroom and stopped doing anything. Zach was suffering with depression and other health deficiencies.

Soon, Zach was connected with a mental health therapist, as well as a medical doctor. With medical and therapeutic interventions, Zach started to feel better. He worked extremely hard through these months to regain his mental and physical health. He also learned skills to recognize when he was struggling and how to take care of himself.

From an incredibly low place of functioning, Zach learned how to keep trying. He learned that it was okay to acknowledge his struggle, accept help, and try different strategies. Most importantly, he learned skills to take care of himself. He found strength from within he did not realize he had—but it was there.

By fall of 2021, Zach returned to in-person learning and officially became a part of his school community. He faced new social stresses and academic challenges but stayed on course to maintain his health and wellness. He knew he could face any next challenges because of what he had experienced and learned about himself.

NEVER, NEVER, NEVER GIVE UP.

These were the words carved into a small brass paperweight that sat on the bookshelf in my school counseling office. I walked by it daily and, admittedly, after many years, looked past its important meaning. A recent graduate, Maggie, reminded me of its importance.

One week following the commencement ceremony, Maggie stopped in to see me one more time before she moved onto her next chapter of life. It was a celebratory conversation mixed with sadness. Maggie came from an unstable family situation with little support. Most of the time, she figured out how to take care of herself but barely.

With minimal guidance around her, Maggie often stayed up all night, and was perpetually tardy to school or missed it altogether. Due to missing school and disengagement, Maggie struggled academically. She needed guidance and support, so she frequently made her way to my office.

Through three years of knowing Maggie, I encouraged every You Can Do Hard Things tool for her to use.

Maggie worked extremely hard through her high school years to find her way. She kept trying . . . and trying. She accepted support from many trusted adults and teachers. There were days she sat slumped in the chair in my office, crying or despondent. It was a roller coaster of moments where Maggie would create an action plan to get back on track, followed by consecutive absences that derailed the plan.

But Maggie kept coming back. She always acknowledged her mistakes and missteps with resolve to do better. Despite the challenging circumstances of her life, she kept trying.

Eventually, Maggie followed through with her action plans, and with one small action after the next, she finally took charge of her schoolwork. She managed to earn passing grades and earn her high school diploma. I was enormously proud of her efforts to keep showing up. And Maggie was immensely proud of herself. It was a celebration!

As Maggie and I sat together for the last time in my office, she kept looking across to the bookshelf where the brass paperweight sat on the shelf. She asked, "Can I take a picture of that?"

She went on to explain, "It means a lot to me because it is what I have always looked at when I've come to your office. It's helped me a lot."

Tears filled my eyes to realize how hard this young woman worked to keep trying to succeed—and she did it! That small paperweight was one of the reminders that kept her going. Through it all, she was the one who persevered. She uncovered strength she didn't realize she had.

There will be challenges.

There will be hard things.

Believe you will find your way.

YOU CAN . . . KEEP TRYING . . . AND TRYING!

TODAY'S ACTION PLAN

Today, how will I keep trying?

Actions for today:

_____

_____

_____

_____

_____

_____

_____

_____

_____

_____

Doodle or draw here . . .

YESTERDAY'S REVIEW

What worked or did not?

What did I learn?

_____

_____

_____

_____

_____

_____

_____

_____

_____

Doodle or draw here . . .

TOMORROW'S ADVENTURE

What will I do again?

What will I do differently?

_____

_____

_____

_____

_____

_____

_____

_____

_____

_____

YOU CAN DO HARD THINGS

Doodle or draw here . . .

CHAPTER FIVE

TOOL #5
YOU CAN . . . TAKE CARE OF YOURSELF!

"Go back and take care of yourself. Your body needs you; your feelings need you; your perceptions need you."
-—Thich Nhat Hanh

Long ago, during my junior year of high school, I ate lots of junk food, spent many late nights with friends, and slept well into the next day. I dozed off in classes, which usually meant I missed the assigned work, which did not help my grades at all. The summer before this school year began, my family had moved from the small city where I had lived all my life. It was a change I looked forward to and I went full steam into it. I arrived at my school with courage and a plan to get involved, make friends, and shine as my real self!

Having never participated in any competitive swimming, a new friend invited me to join the swim team and I enthusiastically accepted. My friend's father also taught me how to ski, I joined a youth group, and I found even more fun. My plan worked; I made friends and was enjoying new experiences. On the swim team, I learned about the challenging work of swim practices while managing school and the rest of my life. It was a year of new adventures. I loved it all . . . and I was exhausted.

I also recognize now that I struggled with some episodes of sadness as I adjusted to the move, family changes, a new school, and my new life. My head and my heart were feeling deeply and processing all the emotions.

Can you relate?

Are you a teen who is trying to manage it all?

By my senior year, I made decisions to manage my life with a more grounded approach, that included creating a better sleep schedule and time management while still having fun. While I enjoyed the swim team experience, I chose to not participate beyond that one year. I focused a little more on my schoolwork, family, friendships, and planning for post-high school. My overall schedule was healthier all-around, with time to rest, reflect, and be real as I focused on the activities and the person I wanted to be.

You may hear self-care being talked about everywhere these days. It turns out, it is truly important to not only physical health but also emotional and mental health.

Research repeatedly points to the three key factors for good health:

· **Sleep**

· **Diet**

· **Exercise**

This information can be found *everywhere*. Look it up. I won't spend time in this book with a lecture and drawn-out facts. You're welcome.

This is the summarized information. The importance of these three points and your emotional, intellectual, physical, and mental health cannot be understated. They are all equally important. If you say you want to succeed in school, sports, extracurricular activities, fun, adventure, and beyond, check yourself on these three key factors. If even just one is not adequate, you are sabotaging your own plan for success.

Answer these questions:

· **How is your sleep? Are you getting at least nine-twelve hours per night?**

· **What do you eat each day? Are you eating a mostly healthy diet?**

· **Are you doing some kind of exercise, like sports, activities, or an individual exercise routine? Are you getting outside?**

If you answered, "Yes, I'm mostly good in all three areas," THAT'S GREAT! Keep doing that and adjust and improve where you can. If you answered, "No, I'm not doing well at all" in any of these three areas, that's okay but decide to do better. You can make small changes that will make a difference.

If you are taking care of your physical health/maintenance, your brain and body will work much better for you. Especially when it comes to mood and mental wellness, you will be able to manage challenging and stressful situations more competently. Your brain will think clearly, be focused, and you will get things done.

How are *you* managing your life?

It is time for you to check your self-care, health, and mental-wellness strategies. This is especially true if you are also going through any difficult life challenges or circumstances.

Here are additional tools and strategies to support positive health and decrease symptoms of stress, anxiety, or depression:

- **Practice mindfulness.** Simply explained, this is the conscious process of pausing, breathing, and being in the present moment. Do this for a few minutes at any time of day. Repeat often.

- **Practice daily journaling.** This includes writing, drawing, or doodling. It's calming and helps to process big feelings.

- **Talk to someone.** This can be a friend, sibling, parent, teacher, coach, school counselor, therapist, or crisis line. (Dial 988 for the National Crisis Line). You are never alone.

- **Practice growth mindset.** There are no mistakes—it's all learning. Learn forward.

- **Practice gratitude.** The more grateful you are, the happier you will be.

Alexa, a high school junior, introduced herself to me with poise and confidence. She told me about her involvement in the service club, her volunteer work in the community, and her goals to go to law school after she graduated. She excelled academically and expressed her determination to be successful.

Within a few weeks of meeting Alexa, I got to know her even more . . . and I began to see a quite different side of her.

My standard questions began to reveal that Alexa slept only a few hours each night. She barely ate anything, and she did nothing for fun since her days were filled with school and volunteer work. She was operating at an elevated level of stress. There were high expectations around everything she believed she needed to accomplish.

One day, she showed up at my office experiencing a full-blown panic attack. Once calm, she explained her anxiety around all social situations at school. These situations caused her incredible distress and were beginning to affect her ability to function.

This student was crumbling, and she had no tools to help herself. She was exhausted, anxious, and stressed about every area of her life. She was either late for school every day or missed classes altogether because of staying up all night with anxiety about completing assignments and preparing for tests. She was desperately trying to keep her head above water while imaginary weights tied to her ankles kept pulling her back down. She was relying solely on her *will* to succeed and was realizing that was falling apart. She had to do something different.

Alexa's family recognized the critical state she was in and helped her to begin a path toward better health routines and mental health support. Alexa had developed fixed habits and a mindset that she believed would lead her to a successful life. The reality was they were harming her and taking her down an extremely unhealthy path.

It was incredible to witness that, by senior year, Alexa was moving toward a healthier lifestyle and sound planning for her future. She accepted help and committed herself to new learning about herself and learning new life tools. I was honored to keep supporting her by being there for her on the many tough days she still endured as she persevered to learn healthier skills and mindset.

Many days, Alexa reached out for help and reminders of the tools she had within to take care of herself. She created *Today Plans*, reviewed *Yesterday Plans,* and revised plans for *Tomorrow's Adventures*. She gave herself permission to reflect and be honest about what was working–and what was not—and to keep moving forward.

One spring day just before final exams and graduation, Alexa popped into my office with an energetic smile. "I feel really good about my upcoming finals!" she confidently stated.

She went on to share how she had been managing preparation for finals while getting enough sleep, eating well, and even hanging out with friends for fun. We high-fived and celebrated with a minute of a happy dance. Alexa sat down momentarily to tell me about her final decisions regarding college and plans post-high school.

She was happy, healthy, and seeing her life path ahead of her. We reflected on the past two years, filled with so much learning about herself. I thanked Alexa for allowing me to support her along her journey. Once again, a young person in front of me showed me how to get through hard things. I was inspired.

Can you relate to Alexa's story?

You can feel better.

*"The only person you should try to be better than
is the person you were yesterday."*
—Matty Mullins

I have met many teens through the years who are operating this way. While there are countless reasons why you may be living with many pressures, you truly can check yourself in these areas of good physical, emotional, and mental wellness. You can take charge of small actions that will improve everything.

Ethan, a high school senior, shared with me that his exercise of choice was walking. He walked to and from school, to social events, or he walked during his free time for relaxation and enjoyment. Ethan even made a choice to not get a driver's license because he enjoyed walking so much.

He rarely accepted rides from his parents or friends. He knew the time he spent walking always helped him to feel more grounded. He would think, organize tasks, or relax in his thoughts. Good for Ethan! This tool will likely be something he uses throughout his lifetime.

What tool are you currently using that is helping you?

Keep doing that!

Mia found herself struggling with the beginning of an eating disorder during her sophomore year of high school. She was spiraling down in the social media world filled with all the unrealistic expectations about how she was supposed to look. Fortunately, when family and friends recognized what was happening, she received mental health support and medical interventions that helped her to move into a healthier mindset around eating and self-image.

She learned more about the negative messaging of social media and chose to stop endlessly scrolling through it. Instead, Mia focused on eating a healthy diet and participating in healthy exercise. She joined sports and activities at school. She was focused and present with who was in front of her—especially herself. She was happy.

Will, a high school junior, loved to play video games. He played for hours and hours each day, usually late into each night. His playtime increased even more when he connected with boys at school who shared the same interest. It felt good to belong to a group. But Will soon recognized the late night routine of playing games was leaving him exhausted to follow through with much of anything else.

He was frequently late to school or missed the days entirely. His grades suffered. His friendships with the other boys began to struggle since he was not at school. Eventually, Will realized he needed to change something. He recognized he did not feel healthy and his participation in daily life was declining. So, Will talked with his friends and discovered many of them were struggling with lack of sleep as well. Together, they made a plan.

As a group, the boys decided to limit their game time and to end at a reasonable curfew each evening. They encouraged each other to make sure homework and other responsibilities did not suffer. Making this plan allowed the boys to continue to participate in an activity they enjoyed together, while maintaining their health and responsibilities.

Make a plan with a friend to check each other on the three pillars of sleep, diet, and exercise.

Support each other!

"It starts with me."

Here are two more tools that are literally all in your head! They contribute in big ways to being happy!

Growth mindset and practicing gratitude.

Use these every day and you will experience an incredible shift to feeling more in control of your life and managing hard things.

"You will always pass failure on your way to success."
-—Mickey Rooney

On a daily basis, I see the relief in students' eyes when they are reassured that it's okay to make a mistake *if* they have a growth mindset.

It's okay to make mistakes!

In fact, it's necessary.

This means you don't have to arrive at high school knowing everything; rather, you can engage more in the experience of learning, which means asking questions, being curious, making mistakes, and learning from them. Sadly, many students and adults live with a fixed mindset.

Here is how they think:

"I can either do it or I can't do it."

Or

"The outcome is predetermined, and my abilities are fixed."

This becomes an uncomfortable box to live in for anyone. It limits growing and it stops effort. "Why should I even try?" With this fixed mindset, it is a sure path to hold yourself back and never try anything new or challenging, and you will absolutely miss out on your potential. Why live with a fixed mindset when you can live with a growth mindset and always see opportunities to learn and grow?

Try thinking this way:

"I can learn to do anything I want!"

"Mistakes help me to learn and improve."

"Through my effort and persistence, I can master anything!"

Take the weight off your shoulders that you must be perfect. Choose to learn what's in front of you. Put effort into really learning; be curious, ask questions, and seek to understand any subject. Allow yourself to make mistakes and learn forward.

Choose gratitude!

The tool of practicing gratitude can become a second nature mindset. Instead of seeing what is negative around you or blaming others for all that seems wrong, choose to look for the positives right in front of you, around you, and within you. The more you practice this simple exercise, the more you will feel a happier mindset and approach to your life. Research repeatedly proves that gratitude empowers you to feel stronger and happier.

Practicing gratitude in my own life has helped me through many tough life circumstances. Now, I weave it into my daily life. I try to move quickly from spending time blaming or whining about what's not working out, to appreciating what is okay and what is within my abilities to improve a tough situation. It's not about dismissing the reality that something is hard, but finding appreciation to build on what is okay. It works.

What are you grateful for?

at the end of the day...
be grateful for what is.

Remember my story about joining the swim team and what I took away from that experience? Applying a growth mindset, I chose to be open to the learning of a new sport. I did not hold onto a fixed mindset that if I didn't excel and win, I would be a failure. Instead, I accepted tips from teammates and my coach and focused on small actions to improve physical conditioning and teamwork. This mindset allowed me to not spend my time with expectations that would cause unnecessary anxiety, stress, and disappointment. I was grateful for the experience in so many ways. I walked away with new learning and new friendships.

Choose to give the tools and strategies from this chapter a try. Change up something in your routine to implement one small action. Keep changing, adding another small action, or reset at any time by reviewing what's helping you to be healthy—or not. You will discover a stronger and healthier you, which will lead you on a stronger path of happiness and success.

You're worth it.

YOU CAN . . . TAKE CARE OF YOURSELF!

TODAY'S ACTION PLAN

Today, what tools will I use to be healthy?

Actions for today:

_____

_____

_____

_____

_____

_____

_____

_____

_____

_____

Doodle or draw here . . .

YESTERDAY'S REVIEW

What worked or did not?

What did I learn?

_____

_____

_____

_____

_____

_____

_____

_____

_____

_____

Doodle or draw here . . .

TOMORROW'S ADVENTURE

What will I do again?

What will I do differently?

_____

_____

_____

_____

_____

_____

_____

_____

_____

_____

Doodle or draw here . . .

CHAPTER SIX

TOOL #6
YOU CAN . . . ASK FOR HELP!

*"Be strong enough to stand alone,
smart enough to know when you need help,
and brave enough to ask for it."*
-—Unknown

It is always okay to ask for help.

Sadly, I have met so many young people (even adults), who are afraid to ask for assistance.

Why? There is a stigma around asking for help. It seems to send the message that one is weak. On the contrary, it's the stronger person who knows they can't get through something hard alone and asks for help.

Whether it's fear, ego, stubbornness, or other reasons, we humans have a hard time when it's time to bring someone else on our team, when it's time to consult with someone else, or when we need another sounding board. This is troubling, and it can be better.

To be clear, my encouragement in all I do to support young people is about finding your own strength, taking charge of your own life, and finding your own way. In fact, the bulk of this book is about just that: sticking with your hard things in life to find a solution that you can take charge of to live your best life. KEEP DOING THAT!

Know, too, that one of the most important ways to take charge of your life may be when you know you need to ask for help. There's a big reason why this chapter needs a big space in this book.

YOU ARE NOT ALONE. YOU ARE NEVER ALONE.

WHEN ANYTHING IN LIFE GETS TOO HARD, ASK FOR HELP!

When you run out of energy, motivation, ideas, or the will to keep going, that's when you absolutely must ask for help. Even before this point, consulting with other supportive people will always help you find clarity and possible solutions.

Jack, a high school sophomore, shared that even though he was afraid at first, he needed help managing his feelings around his parents' divorce. He knew he was struggling with his own confused, sad, and angry feelings, especially toward his dad. He felt his dad had caused much of the trouble within their family.

Everything hurt so much regarding the chaos in Jack's home—especially how his parents were struggling and the changes that were taking place. He knew he needed his own support to help himself. So, he did something different, something he could take charge of, and he asked for help.

At first, it seemed easier to not bother anyone and keep all his mixed-up feelings to himself. But as time went on, he felt as though he might explode with everything he was keeping inside. He couldn't sleep, he wasn't eating well, and he was losing his motivation to do anything at all. He knew he had to do something when he noticed his inability to have conversations with even his closest friends.

I encouraged Jack to make a plan to talk with his mom and let her know he was struggling. He told her, "I'm worried about me." She was relieved that Jack had finally said something out loud since she had been very worried about him. She sat down and listened to him.

Jack felt an enormous grip release from his body. He felt like he could breathe a little bit better; that he had been holding everything in. She suggested it might be helpful to talk with a therapist about what was going on in his life. He was terrified but eager to see if this feeling of new breathing could feel even better. Jack found a safe space with a therapist. Being open to therapy helped him to learn valuable life skills of expressing feelings and taking care of himself. He would certainly take these skills with him through life.

Jack was fortunate that his mother understood he was asking for help. He was fortunate that the therapist he met was able to provide exactly the support he needed. It was a positive experience, and he learned more about himself. He was able to navigate his parents' divorce with better coping strategies.

Choosing to seek therapy is a courageous step. This process may or may not go smoothly. If you are seeking therapy, stick with the process until you find an arrangement that supports you. It will be worth your efforts. If therapy is not an attainable option, talk with your school counselor about other ways to get support.

"Don't let this darkness fool you.
All lights turned off can be turned on.
—Noah Kahan

I came to know a student named Maria when I was the school counselor at her elementary school. One sunny afternoon in my office, Maria stayed back to talk with just me following a small friendship group session with her and her classmates. "I'm afraid of people," Maria confessed. "I have problems because of things that have happened to me."

She explained that she knew she was struggling with making friends and interacting with teachers. She didn't trust anyone. While she was far from understanding her fear, she knew she wanted it to feel better.

So, she asked me for help.

She explained that she had been sexually abused by a family friend two years before. She'd moved in with her loving grandmother. Everyone thought the traumatic incident was behind them, but Maria continued to struggle as she grew older.

Until that moment, I could have never imagined the terrifying world Maria was living in. My heart hurt as I realized how much she had suffered. She was stuck and afraid.

I was grateful that Maria decided I was a safe person to finally ask for help. I am honored to have held this similar space for many young people as they finally said out loud about the hard things in their lives. I am proud of their courage and their determination to find happiness.

I was able to help Maria get connected with a therapist who could help her work through her trauma. The therapist was able to help Maria develop more positive coping strategies and find courage to trust relationships again. She visited the therapist once a week throughout that entire school year.

A few years later, I passed Maria in the hallway of the neighborhood high school where I arrived for a professional development meeting. She was walking with several friends, and she was smiling and laughing. When she spotted me, she smiled even bigger and waved. We didn't stop to talk since she appeared to be rushing with her friends to get somewhere.

I sent back to her my big smile and unspoken message: "I see you are happy and that's all I need to see. You worked very hard to get to this point. Good job." I walked on to my meeting, feeling gratitude for the opportunities I have had to be in these spaces to support young people.

Sophia, a new freshman student, found herself completely overwhelmed with entering the high school environment. She was excited and wanted to get off to a great start. She made a smart decision to ask for help at the beginning of the school year. Sophia and I checked in regularly and talked about strategies to succeed in high school: how to talk with teachers, hone her study skills, develop time management, and get involved in extracurricular activities.

Sophia quickly took charge of her academics and got involved in sports and clubs. Her confidence increased and it showed to everyone else. She made friends and was happy. She reduced many possible days of struggle and stress by recognizing immediately that she needed extra support around this transition to high school and asked for help.

Asking for help and establishing your support people go a long way toward helping you to keep moving forward. Don't miss the chance to feel supported by someone.

Let's normalize asking for help.

If you do not feel safe with yourself, ASK FOR HELP IMMEDIATELY.

If you are harming yourself, someone is harming you, or you are thinking of harming someone else, ASK FOR HELP IMMEDIATELY.

If you are struggling with your emotions, daily functioning, relationships, or not moving forward the way you would like, ASK FOR HELP.

If you are having any thoughts about suicide, ASK FOR HELP IMMEDIATELY.

If you need to share what you are thinking inside of your head and need a sounding board, ASK SOMEONE TO BE THAT PERSON.

Reach out to a trusted adult, a parent, school counselor, teacher, coach, or other adult who you know cares about you. They will know if they are the person qualified to help you, or they will know how to connect you with someone else.

DIAL 988 (National Crisis Line) ANY TIME OF DAY!

This 24/7 national crisis line is staffed with trained crisis counselors who will listen to you and help. They will be your sounding board. There is always someone who will listen to you.

I highly encourage you to learn to say the words, "I need help." That will always get the most direct response and immediate help. But I get it; sometimes you may not know what you really need. So, find someone to talk with and describe what you are feeling. They will be able to help you make sense of your feelings and help you find your direction.

Tell me your story. I'm listening.

"When I was a boy and I would see scary things in the news, my mother would say to me, 'Look for the helpers. You will always find people who are helping.'"
-—Mr. Fred Rogers

Jared asked for help to manage his academics better after he acknowledged how much he was struggling. Gilbert, feeling overwhelming sadness, finally opened up to his school counselor about the death of his mother. Caroline asked for help with ideas to navigate a difficult friendship. Max asked for help when he knew he was struggling with his mental health but didn't know what to do. Victoria broke down with a flood of emotions as she said, "I don't know what I need!"

These are young people who didn't necessarily know what they needed, but they needed someone else to listen.

Once a conversation begins, it's amazing how quickly solutions or plans can be implemented. Help can happen fast. Feeling better almost immediately follows—or at least relief that there are next steps—and that's better than if you never asked for help.

All the chapters of this book are designed to empower you with tools to feel stronger, more confident, and more in control of your life path. As you strengthen in all areas and use these life tools, you will gain a better sense of when you need to ask for help. You will skip any uncertainty or judgment if it's the right thing to do because you will remind yourself you are not alone. You will always need positive, supportive people around you.

YOU CAN . . . ASK FOR HELP!

TODAY'S ACTION PLAN

Today, who can I ask for help?

Actions for today:

_____

_____

_____

_____

_____

_____

_____

_____

_____

_____

Doodle or draw here . . .

YESTERDAY'S REVIEW

What worked or did not?

What did I learn?

Doodle or draw here . . .

TOMORROW'S ADVENTURE

What will I do again?

What will I do differently?

Doodle or draw here . . .

CHAPTER SEVEN

TOOL #7
YOU CAN . . . BEGIN AGAIN!

"I've failed over and over and over again in my life.
And that is why I succeed."
-—Michael Jordan

Mistakes are an important part of learning. Embrace them. Choose to learn forward. Choose to keep trying. Don't give up before you allow yourself the opportunity to reach an even greater outcome.

I say to students every day: "You didn't arrive at high school with perfect knowledge of calculus, chemistry, history, writing, or accomplishments in sports, music, or art. You are not expected to be an expert in relationships or knowing how to do a job. You're learning! In fact, it will be a lifetime of learning."

Get out of your head that you're supposed to know it all and do everything perfectly.

Get into your head the mindset that you will learn from your mistakes and will always take away learning from everything you do.

If you failed a test in any subject, use the growth mindset tool. See where you made a mistake, where you didn't prepare well enough, and how you will improve next time. Talk with your teacher and ask, "Could you please help me with understanding what I got wrong on the test?" Better yet, before an upcoming test, ask, "How should I prepare for this test? What concepts and/ or study strategies do you recommend?" Then take those recommendations and do better.

If you didn't write your best essay, then review, revise, and rewrite it. All writers go through many drafts before finalizing their best words.

If you messed up on an art project or musical piece you've been practicing, go back and try it again. Focus on the places that need more effort. Keep doing that!

If you reacted and said something mean to a friend, go back, own your mistake, apologize, and say how you'll manage your reaction better next time.

If you fell through with your own self-care routine of exercising, eating well, and following your sleep schedule, forgive yourself, resolve to do better, and make a new plan for tomorrow.

This may be hard to believe, but when you make a mistake, you will increase your confidence when you acknowledge it and set your mind toward improvement next time. If you allow your ego and expectations of perfection drive you, you will always feel disappointed with yourself. Beware of the *shoulds*.

"I should do it perfectly."

"I should never fail."

"I should look perfect."

"I should always get everything right."

The *shoulds* will always be a set-up for disappointment. You will never reach perfection– nobody will. You will end up feeling anxiety, stress, and exhaustion while chasing an unattainable goal. You will never feel satisfied.

Instead, create a world around you where you allow yourself grace to make mistakes and learn from them. Begin again.

Take away the blame, erase the *shoulds*, then bounce back and begin again. There truly is no other option if you want to succeed in anything. Get humble and take charge; you'll thank yourself later when you realize you are stronger to handle the next mistake because there will always be one.

We're messy humans and we mess up.

We're real.

Let's get stronger at beginning again.

That's how we do better.

That's how we succeed.

As I talked with Andrew, a high school sophomore, he confidently shared with me, "I want my grades to look good, all *A* grades." With one year of high school behind him, Andrew had grasped the importance of doing his best. He had plans for a successful future. He knew that to get into a good college, he would need an impressive high school transcript.

Andrew went on to explain, "I am trying so hard to get a good grade in calculus."

"Is it a challenging class?" I asked him.

"Yes, it's very hard; it's the hardest class I've ever taken. I just don't get it!" Andrew stated with a rising tone. "It's so stressful. I freak out before every test because I don't think I'm going to do well. I make lots of mistakes when I realize I didn't study well enough."

"How do you study for this class?" I asked Andrew.

Andrew gave me a confused look and shrugged, "I don't know, kind of like the way I study for all of my classes; I just read through my notes."

To clarify, I asked gently, "So, this is the hardest class you've ever taken, you just don't get it, yet you're using the same study strategy you use with all of your other classes? And then you're upset when you don't get an *A* grade?" I carefully suggested to Andrew, "What if you need a different approach to study and understand this particular subject?"

Andrew's eyes widened. He seemed to be considering this new idea as if he was thinking, *So, it's not that I am dumb and will never understand this subject? I just need to change how I study?*

Andrew suddenly seemed to see an opening where he could take charge of learning a different way and improve the outcome of his math grade. He had to move on from beating himself up, be okay with the mistakes he had made, find understanding, and approach this subject in a different way. Andrew was energized by this plan when he realized he could take charge and succeed in this class. He decided he would meet with his teacher to get input on better study strategies. He was hopeful. Once Andrew acknowledged he had something to learn, he was able to begin again with a stronger mindset and approach.

Lydia, a high school junior, found herself in a huge social mess. She sat in my office crying about how she had messed up with making friends. She had been focusing on one friend group that she believed was the "popular group" that she needed to be a part of. She was constantly unhappy with herself and frustrated with the other girls. She told me how the group spent endless hours gossiping, scrolling through social media, texting stupid memes, and they were constantly mean to other students. Lydia was interested in playing sports, joining clubs, and participating in school activities, but she couldn't get anyone else to join her. She was letting these frustrations be known to the group, which was increasingly distancing her from them.

As Lydia talked more, she came to realize she was trying to be part of a group of friends that just weren't her fit. Lydia decided she could keep feeling unhappy or she could choose to begin again with a new plan for herself.

I asked Lydia to make a list of her positive qualities, interests, and how she wanted to show up as a friend. Her list revealed a genuine, caring person with an enthusiasm for getting involved in new activities.

She planned to research clubs at the school and join the next season's sport. Lydia developed a plan to let her current friends know she would stay in touch but would be trying some new things. (This approach also minimized the potential drama since she was not attacking anyone.) She was excited and nervous at the same time to be doing something different. She was proud of herself for beginning again with a new plan.

"It is better to be yourself and have no friends than to be like your friends and have no self."
-—QuoteDiary.me

How you begin again in any area of your life will be unique to you. Only you can make this decision. It will likely take a huge leap of courage, but it's worth it when you discover new learning, new success, or new fun!

Do you need to begin again?

Beginning again gives you permission to always keep trying, keep exploring, and uncovering a stronger YOU. You will learn from mistakes, be more resilient, and be inevitably more successful because you will know how to manage setbacks, revise plans, and keep moving forward. This is most definitely a lifetime skill! Get good at beginning again!

YOU CAN . . . BEGIN AGAIN TODAY

TODAY'S ACTION PLAN

Today, how will I begin again?

Actions for today:

_____

_____

_____

_____

_____

_____

_____

_____

_____

_____

Doodle or draw here . . .

YESTERDAY'S REVIEW

What worked or did not?

What did I learn?

_____

_____

_____

_____

_____

_____

_____

_____

_____

_____

Doodle or draw here . . .

TOMORROW'S ADVENTURE

What will I do again?

What will I do differently?

_____

_____

_____

_____

_____

_____

_____

_____

_____

_____

Doodle or draw here . . .

CHAPTER EIGHT

TOOL #8
YOU CAN . . . CREATE YOUR LIFE!

"The purpose of our lives is to be happy."
-—Dalai Lama

You get to take charge of your life!

Create the life of your dreams. Own it. You are not in this world to live someone else's life. Do not let anyone or anything influence you to become someone you are not. Embrace this journey. You will travel to happy places, terrifying places, and challenging places, all of which will help you become a stronger and amazing YOU! Be courageous, remain open, and always take away learning. This is *your* life. Make it *your* journey.

Identify your values and your own compass. A compass is a device that determines accurate directions by means of a magnetic needle. Imagine you have your own compass where the magnetic needle will always pull you back to your values and true self. Maybe these are values from your family, your faith, or another life model. Define the person you want to become and start exploring and building YOU.

When times get hard, *and there will be hard times,* return to your compass. Stay true to it and you will feel more secure, in control, and grounded. You will be more confident to take chances and experience new things.

At some time, you will feel the pressures of others who want to tell you who you should be. This is awesome advice if you align with their advice. However, if you feel someone is attempting to pull you away from your compass and your values, then take time to consider your best direction.

Others may play every skillful card to convince you of a better path. It may be something shiny and new, which may attract your attention for a bit, and you may even consider this the way you want to go. If this feels like your path and aligns with your compass, then go for it. But if you feel any reservation that something is not in alignment, pause and consider if this is your best path.

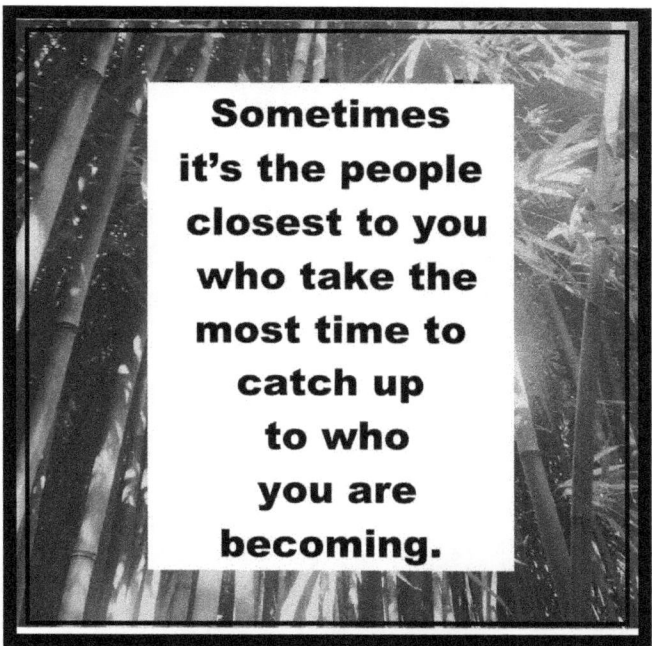

It's a gut feeling. It's hard to explain but start noticing when you get "a feeling" that something doesn't seem right. Choose to pause and think a little more about what's best for you.

"You have to believe in yourself when no one else does . . . that makes you a winner right there."
-—Venus Williams

Plan accordingly. Follow the tools from this book and return to them frequently as reminders to you that you can do hard things. Your life experiences, bumps, or obstacles in the road will make you stronger. When you allow your compass to be your guide, you will feel more secure in charting an amazing life for yourself.

Fast forward to your adult life. I have been fortunate to stay connected with young people I've known through their teen years and now into their adult lives. They are each on their own journey and creating their own path, complete with beginnings, revisions, beginning agains, and beyond.

Evolve while traveling on your path.

When you become an adult, you will be free to truly uncover your true self. Give yourself permission to explore and identify the paths you would like to travel. Return to your compass, expand, and strengthen it, and keep learning about yourself.

If the path you're on is no longer your path, change it!

My daughter, Megan, couldn't wait for her next chapter to begin following high school. She made her choice to attend a D1 university on the East Coast, enroll in a five-year nursing program, and swim competitively. She had always thrived on a busy schedule and felt confident she could manage it all. Upon arrival, Megan was also invited to join the crew team. She accepted the invitation.

Three years later, she decided to change her path. She worked incredibly hard to maintain an almost incomprehensible schedule of classes, nurse clinical rotations at hospitals, swim and crew practices, race events, and a work-study job. There truly were not enough hours in each day to accomplish everything she had signed up to do. Her physical and mental health were suffering. She missed her home and family. Ultimately, she was supported by her family to consider how her path needed to change.

Nothing was a mistake. Megan would take away tremendous learning. She returned to her childhood home and began again in another nursing school program at the nearby university. She completed the program with high honors and easily found employment as a registered nurse. Megan realized tremendous growth, strength, and learning about herself that she likely would not have even come close to had she not faced these challenges.

Welcome to your adult life!

You will likely change your path many times over.

Take away learning from every experience.

Learn. Grow. Repeat.

While you are still in high school, dream about your future, create goals, and make plans. Change your direction when you must. This is *not at all* about encouraging you to quickly bail when things get tough. Know they will get tough, and you will likely find yourself outside of your comfort zone.

Keep your goals ahead of you and learn to recognize the effort needed to reach them. Work hard and stay the course if this is the path you need to reach your goals. You will tap into the perseverance needed to achieve great things. Use your support system of positive people to be your sounding board. Listen to them and yourself. Choose wisely.

I know many former students who entered their adult life paths with determination to either build on successes of high school or resolve to improve from past struggles. They're all finding their way.

Noah struggled academically in high school and barely earned his diploma. Learning from his past mistakes, he was determined to create a stronger academic path for himself. He entered college and began using more positive and healthy life tools for success.

During her high school years, Isla had wanted desperately to be a part of student government, but she was never elected to office. Still sure of her passion to contribute to her school, community, and causes, Isla joined the university student government groups where she thrived.

Logan experienced success easily throughout high school but found college to be extremely challenging. He considered quitting school. Before he made this decision, he sought out supportive guidance from an academic advisor on campus, reflected on his true compass, and allowed himself to explore new areas of interest. He discovered a new focus of study and adventures that would all eventually connect with his future career and happier life.

Carter, diagnosed with learning differences since his childhood, would not allow these challenges to prevent him from earning a higher education degree. When he arrived at college, he immediately sought out resources and support. He graduated with a high honors bachelor's degree and set his path to earn a graduate level degree.

What path do you see traveling in your adult life?

As we know by now, life paths are rarely straight and smooth. In fact, it's the turns and bumps in the road that will likely strengthen you the most while opening your eyes to possibilities and adventures. But along the way, you may get tired and feel impatient when your path isn't falling into place. Choose to persevere and see your goals ahead of you. They may be just around the bend.

My daughter, Marisa, shared a dream she had during a challenging time when her adult life path felt unclear. She was unsure of her next best decision. During a restless night of sleep, Marisa heard her beloved late grandfather's comforting voice in her dream. He gently said, "You can keep going." A sense of relief and renewed strength wrapped around her. She awoke to a new day. She said to herself, "I can do this!" Marisa kept going, and she continues to evolve as she travels her unique life path.

Always remember you are built to do hard things.

During tough periods, remind yourself to return to the life tools from this book. Ground yourself. Strengthen yourself. Believe in yourself.

You can do hard things, and you will find your way.

Be open to where your path may lead you.

So, while you are still in your teen years, do your best, be kind to yourself, and always be open to learning. Explore the possibilities of your future adult life. You'll be there before you know it. Seek support and help from a school counselor, college counselor, parents, or other trusted adults. Design a plan that is realistic and achievable, but remember, it does not have to be perfect. Just make a plan. See yourself becoming your best self or at least evolving along your journey. It will take a lifetime. Keep doing that.

Keep learning and becoming a better you.

Let the stories of the young people within this book inspire you.

Their stories are courageous examples of getting through hard things.

Embrace your path and your journey.

Nobody else can design your path for you.

You get to create your life.

You have a lifetime.

You've got this.

YOU CAN . . . CREATE YOUR LIFE!

Take care. I believe in you. MKB

TODAY'S ACTION PLAN

Who do I want to become?

How will I get there?

Actions for today:

_____

_____

_____

_____

_____

_____

_____

_____

_____

_____

Doodle or draw here . . .

YESTERDAY'S REVIEW

What worked or did not?

What did I learn?

_____

_____

_____

_____

_____

_____

_____

_____

_____

Doodle or draw here . . .

TOMORROW'S ADVENTURE

What will I do again?

What will I do differently?

_____

_____

_____

_____

_____

_____

_____

_____

_____

_____

Doodle or draw here . . .

YOU CAN . . . TALK WITH YOUR PARENTS!

When you have healthy parents or guardians who support you, but they may not seem to understand you (or you them), is it possible to become a more united team?

Somedays you may feel like you and your parents are a winning team, while other days you may feel like you're sitting out on the bench. It's worth everyone's effort to work together to be a cohesive and united team. It takes learning and practice for any team to do well. Take charge of your position on the team. Help your parents to understand you, and they will know better how to support you.

Try something different . . .

Write a letter to your parents and say what you need to say. Get your thoughts out of your head and onto this paper. Maybe you will choose to share this letter with a parent . . . or not. Maybe your thoughts will become talking points for a conversation face-to-face. You decide. What if your parents could understand you a little more, and you could learn a little more about them? Have courage.

What are the possibilities if you become a stronger team?

Below are some prompts to guide you in your writing. You can also choose to your own words exactly how you need to say them.

Writing Prompts:

- I am a work-in-progress and trying to learn about myself every day . . .

- Some days I feel courage while other days I'm afraid . . .

- I am discovering who I need to become . . .

- Some days I want to give up, but I keep trying . . .

- I want to learn to be healthy and manage my life well . . .

- I want to take charge and do things on my own, but sometimes I need to ask for help . . .

- I make mistakes and mess up; this is how I learn . . .

- I want to grow up, get out into the world, and be happy, healthy, and successful . . .

- I want to become my best self. I don't know who that is yet, but I am on my own path . . .

- What I need to do by myself is . . .

- What I need help with is . . .

Dear Mom, Dad, or Guardian,

_____

_____

_____

_____

_____

_____

_____

_____

_____

_____

_____

Doodle or draw here . . .

MY LETTER TO PARENTS

"It's not what you do for your children but what you have taught them to do for themselves that will make them successful beings."
-—Ann Landers

You can . . . let your teen do hard things!

You must allow your teen to do hard things!

This is my letter to you, parent-to-parent. I get it because I'm a parent too. I've also been watching parents support their children for over forty years through various professional settings. I know it's not easy. I've heard it said that parenting is the hardest job.

It was certainly a tough job for my husband and me to raise our two daughters, *and* it was fun, terrifying, challenging, difficult, amazing, and beautiful all at the same time. We made many mistakes, but hopefully we did some things right too. Most of all, we hope we prepared them enough to embrace life to the fullest, do good things for the world, and learn the skills to face the hard things.

As adults and parents, we are all navigating our own individual paths and our own hard things while also helping our children to grow, learn skills, and discover their own paths. Take care of yourself on this journey.

The world around our teens is more complicated than ever and moving faster than ever due to technology and the speed of information. They are surrounded 24/7 by social media platforms, constant communication expectations (texting and apps), games, and social pressures. They are flooded with continuous messaging (reality or not), that says who they should be, look like, perform like, feel like, identify as, causes to fight for, *and* they're supposed to have this all figured out in their adolescent years.

Add in just a little more of any other possible life challenges or difficult circumstances, and it's overwhelming for them. There's a lot happening around them, and they need life tools to manage it all.

You are the most important life tool for your children.

From my school counselor office, I have observed young people searching for their way to learn about themselves and find their life path. I have seen genuine determination to do the best they can but not always knowing how to do it. Most of the time, they know when they've made a mistake and when they've done something well. They thrive when they are surrounded by parents who notice their efforts and learning, who won't give up on them, who allow them to make mistakes, and who support them to learn their own life lessons.

I have heard this expressed in countless different ways, but these phrases pretty much sum up what I hear from young people toward their parents:

Let me try to do it on my own . . . but stay close.

Let me make choices . . . but stay close.

When I make mistakes, let me figure it out . . . but stay close.

When I need to talk, please listen . . . and stay close.

Stay close.

As they travel their own paths to uncover who they need to be for the world, be the adult who stays close while they travel. Be the adult who models facing your own hard things and using healthy life tools to get through them. If you don't know how, seek learning for yourself. How you navigate your own path will always be the most powerful learning for your children.

Encourage your teen:

- **To explore.**

- **To problem-solve.**

- **To make mistakes.**

- **To learn.**

- **To begin again.**

- **To take charge.**

Don't attempt to create a perfect world around your teen where they never experience challenges or feeling uncomfortable. Allow them to experience feeling their own feelings. Don't take that away from them. When they feel a big feeling, encourage them to notice it and allow them space to choose how to manage it.

Allow them to try their own ideas or tools. If necessary, offer an idea or tool that may help . . . and stay close. Celebrate when they find their own tools and ways to get through hard things. See their confidence and sense of self grow when they realize they can take charge of tough situations.

Support them when their ideas or tools don't work; encourage them to try again. Help them to understand this is real life. Again, show them how *you* manage real life.

They need to experience their own problems and challenges. They need to experience making their own decisions and outcomes, good or bad. They need to feel their own successes *and* their own failures.

Let this happen!

When they stick with their own problem, they will find their own solution, and they will feel the satisfaction of figuring it all out, or they will feel the disappointment of not figuring it all out. It will all be okay. Either way, their sense of self and responsibility will increase when they face the next problem.

Before you know it, they will be more independent and able to persevere through hard things. They will know they can find their way through life. You will feel reassured that they can do it!

Let these challenges happen while they are young, and you are nearby to encourage and support them. Your unconditional love and never-ending encouragement will always be the right parenting techniques.

Stay close.

YOU CAN . . . LET YOUR TEEN DO HARD THINGS!

*"Of all the paths you take in life,
make sure a few of them are dirt."*
—John Muir

ABOUT THE AUTHOR

Kay Bush is an author, school counselor, and youth mental health first aid instructor.

Author of two books, *Alberta Lee Wareing Blue: Her Stories* and *You Can Do Hard Things: Life Tools for Teens,* Kay learns from the life stories of real people. Whether compiling her mother's memories of her life or the stories of young people, Kay is an empathic listener and life-long learner of people.

For over forty years, with education in psychology, child and family development, and school counseling, Kay has been listening to the stories of young people. She has supported teens and children in hospitals, support groups, and educational settings. From these spaces, Kay learned how teens get through tough life situations. Courage, belief mindset, skills of perseverance, and resilience are the tools that empower young people to take charge of their circumstances.

As a certified youth mental health first aid instructor, Kay teaches adults to recognize signs and symptoms of mental health challenges in teens and how to offer first-responder care.

Kay is the founder of the You Can Do Hard Things project, an online platform that encourages youth to share their stories of challenges and how they found their strength through them. Their stories are the inspiration for other teens to uncover their strength, keep moving forward, and know they are never alone.

Kay welcomes all conversations around empowering youth. Please reach out.

If you are a teen and have a tough life story, and found the strength to continue your path, you may be the inspiration for another teen. Please share your story.

Website: www.YouCanDoHardThings.today

Instagram: @_youcandohardthings

Email: youcandohardthings.today@gmail.com

REVIEWS

"You Can Do Hard Things is a wonderful book for making yourself better. With stories and real experiences that show you that you can improve, it helps make it a go-to when talking about self-help and overcoming challenges. I would recommend this book to anybody trying to change their life for the better."
   —Mace, 13 year old

"Kay has truly heard the call of what our nation's youth have needed! In her book, it's clear she has written from her heart and many years of experience working to support youth in their challenges. While beautifully written and enormously hopeful for teens, counselors will also find this book an effective, useful tool in guiding adolescents to be inspired to reach their potential! It would be a great prerequisite reading for emerging adults!"
   —Valerie Huff, MSS, LCSW
   Psychotherapist, Main Line Health, King of Prussia, Pennsylvania

"You Can Do Hard Things is a book that every teen and anyone should read to know they are more able and courageous to handle hard things. It is an easy read with worksheets to help implement the tools. Reading stories you can relate to makes the book feel like you are not alone. The entire book feels like you have a best friend talking to you. This book will change lives. It is a must-read for anyone, especially teens!!"

—Terry Sidford, TedX Speaker, Author, Coach Owner of Create Your Life International

"Do not be fooled by the title that suggests the book is for teens! M. Kay Bush. You Can Do Hard Things is a tool every person can use. The examples she uses demonstrate not only the what, but also the how of developing a healthy lifestyle of purpose, freedom, and happiness. I would recommend this book to all who want a 'growing' life."

—Elda Robinson, International Best Selling author of One More Thing...

"You Can Do Hard Things: Life Tools for Teens by M. Kay Bush is an empowering guide that equips teenagers with practical strategies to overcome challenges and achieve their goals. Through relatable stories of real-life teens, Bush inspires readers to adopt a positive mindset, take proactive steps, and build resilience. The book's interactive approach encourages self-reflection and personal growth, covering topics such as

goal setting, self-care, and relationships. Written in a conversational tone, it fosters a sense of camaraderie and support, reassuring teens that they are not alone in their struggles. Overall, it's a compelling resource for any teen seeking inspiration and guidance."

—Kristin Kladis, PhD
Director of Student Services, Judge Memorial Catholic High School

"This powerful book is part workbook, part journal, part book of quotes and part step-by-step guide to getting through life's challenges. The eight tools are illustrated through the use of stories that teens will find relatable and be able to see themselves in. These seemingly simple tools are explained using easy-to-understand language and immediately applicable strategies. Every young person should read this book. I wish I had had it when I was a teen."

—Michele Pilon, Washington Wellness with Michele Mental Health Instructor, Consultant, and Coach

"The value in this book is its straightforward, common sense, skill building approach. Real-life examples that span the wide range of the adolescent experience make the book applicable to most teens. The phrase 'you can do hard things' implies a growth mindset. That life is not static. That hard times or struggles do not last forever. That each of us is equipped to learn the skills needed to do those hard things.

I really appreciate the 'but you just haven't found it... yet' phrase that is used in the book. The dots between 'it' and 'yet' might just be the most important part of that line. The dots offer possibility. And ideas. And space for learning. None of us are equipped with all the answers all the time. It keeps our focus on a growth mindset and how it can start with little things.

As a manager, one of the themes I've seen with young staff members is that they think they should know everything on day one of the job and they look at new situations as failure vs learning opportunities. We talk about that a fair amount. Teens do this same thing. And worse, they believe they are the only one who doesn't know all the things; so asking for help required setting pride aside. Easier said than done.

Speaking from a voice that is sometimes school counselor, sometimes child life specialist, sometimes parent, sometimes teen lifts up the author's humanity as well as vast experience."

—Kristen C. Quinn, M.Ed., CMHC, CCLS
Behavioral Sciences Manager, Social Work and Spiritual Care Department, University of Utah Health

"M. Kay Bush's book was so inspiring and helped me so much with my anxiety and depression. I recommend this book to any reader who is suffering from any sort of mental illness. The great stories were so inspiring and amazing and kept me reading all the way to the end.

This book also helped me get through some of my anxiety and it let me work on, not only my physical life, but on my mental life too! I highly recommend this book to anyone! Thank you for letting me read this book."
—Maren, 12 year old

"Experienced school counselor M. Kay Bush avoids getting bogged down in the long list of modern challenges for young people in this accessible and straight-talking resilience guide for teens. Instead, You Can Do Hard Things uses simple advice and relatable counselor's office case studies, to bring the focus back to basics. Her simple, encouraging advice challenges teens to focus on what they can control, with courage, authenticity, self-care, and persistence. Her eight-step tool kit and planning templates could be game changers for overwhelmed teens."
—Mary Bolling, Australian parenting podcaster, Gotta Be Done-A Bluey Podcast

"In You Can Do Hard Things, Bush offers a practical toolkit that empowers teens to better recognize and harness their inherent potential. Through potent prose, compelling anecdotes, and personal experiences interwoven throughout, Bush constructs a step-by-step framework accessible to teenagers from all walks of life. In today's post-pandemic- landscape, marked by heightened anxiety, social media saturation, and persistent societal divisions, You Can Do Hard Things

presents invaluable resources for teenagers and parents alike to navigate challenging subjects with expert guidance and actionable tools."
   —Matthew Douglas, Ph.D. Candidate
   Dean of Students, Judge Memorial Catholic High School, Salt Lake City, UT

"If you need a 'Can Do' book for a teenager in your life, You Can Do Hard Things is packed with life tools and strategies. Not only will it assist your teen to overcome challenges and uncover unique strengths, it will support them to meet their goals. It is a great way to assist your teenager to take charge, and become a happier, more powerful version of themselves."
   —Lyn T. Christian - Founder of SoulSalt Inc. and Best-Selling Author

"Kay Bush is a highly skilled school counselor that has made it her life mission to support students in need. She has the ability to find the glimmer of hope in some of the most challenging moments. Her well-written book brings her decades of experience to help the reader become actively engaged in their journey for improved mental health. This book is an incredible tool for those who are looking for positive support as a student, teacher, counselor, coach, mentor, or parent."
   —Patrick Lambert, M.S. Ed.

"M. Kay Bush's book, *You Can Do Hard Things: Life Tools for Teens* is a must-read for anyone who is looking to reach their goals and approach life with a positive outlook.

As someone who strives to maintain a positive outlook, I found it to be truly inspiring.

You CAN DO hard things! Change starts with that first step. Need motivation? Read this powerful book and I guarantee you'll be motivated! Everyone can use a few more life tools to help them along the way!!"

—Misti Mazurik, Director of Operations, RHG Media Productions

"*You Can Do Hard Things* is a motivational guide empowering teens to navigate challenges with optimism, fostering resilience and courage."

—Maureen Ryan Blake, Maureen Ryan Blake Media

"Wow! Kay has taken years of personal and professional experience and translated that into actionable items for young people, with lessons along the way. This is the book I wish I had twenty-five years ago!

Kay accesses the lived experience of both she and the young people she has collaborated with to share essential life lessons with those on the cusp of their next step. Any young person and their grownups would benefit from this book!

Thank you, Kay, for turning your experience into action-able items for young people and their grown-ups to consider and guide their next steps!"
—Sunny Noelle Naughton, Sunshine Silver Lining